Titles in this series
*Don't Call Me Special* – a first look at disability
*I Can Be Safe* – a first look at safety
*I Miss You* – a first look at death
*Is It Right to Fight?* – a first look at anger
*My Amazing Body* – a first look at health and fitness
*My Brother, My Sister, and Me* – a first look at sibling rivalry
*My Family's Changing* – a first look at family break-up
*My Friends and Me* – a first look at friendship
*My New Family* – a first look at adoption
*Stop Picking on Me* – a first look at bullying
*The Skin I'm In* – a first look at racism

First edition for the United States and Canada published in 2003 by Barron's Educational Series, Inc.

First edition for Great Britain published 2003 by Hodder Wayland, an imprint of Hodder Children's Books under the title *Is It Right to Fight? A First Look at Conflict*.

Text © Pat Thomas 2003
Illustrations © Lesley Harker 2003

*All inquiries should be addressed to:*
Barron's Educational Series, Inc.
250 Wireless Boulevard
Hauppauge, New York 11788
*http://www.barronseduc.com*

Library of Congress Catalog Card No. 2002111581

ISBN-13: 978-0-7641-2458-7

Manufactured by: Shenzhen Wing King Tong Paper Products Co. Ltd.
Shenzhen, Guangdong, China.
September 2013

Printed and bound in China
16  15  14  13  12  11

# Is It Right to Fight?

**A FIRST LOOK AT ANGER**

**PAT THOMAS**
**ILLUSTRATED BY LESLEY HARKER**

Have you ever been so mad that you
wanted to yell or scream or even
hit someone?

Maybe someone said something mean to you
or broke one of your favorite toys. Perhaps you
got blamed for something you did not do.

Everyone feels angry sometimes. It is okay to feel angry.

Sometimes it is even a good thing, because when
you are treated unfairly, anger can give you
the courage to speak out.

But hitting and screaming, or *acting out* anger, is never helpful. It always makes things worse. But *talking out* anger can help to resolve a situation.

## What about you?

Have you ever had a fight or an argument with someone? What did you fight about? Did fighting solve the problem?

Sometimes it is fun to have a play fight.

It can also be fun to play games or watch programs where people fight but do not get hurt.

But real fighting is never that much fun. It also helps to remember that disagreements can usually be resolved long before the fighting point.

Fighting can make you so upset that your head and stomach start to hurt.

It can make it hard to sleep or sit still.

If you hit someone or hurt their feelings it
can make you feel sad and ashamed.
But talking out conflicts in ways
that don't cause you or the other
person to get hurt is good.

People fight for lots of different reasons. They fight when they are feeling angry, or scared, or hurt and left out.

Some people fight because they think it makes them look big and strong.

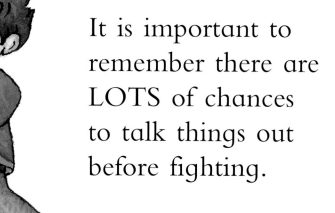

It is important to remember there are LOTS of chances to talk things out before fighting.

Being around people who are always fighting
can make you feel very unhappy.

Sometimes a friend might ask you to help them fight with others. Other times someone may pick a fight with you for no reason you can understand.

When this happens you may end up fighting
even if you do not really want to.

## What about you?

Has this ever happened to you? Can you
think of some ways to avoid fighting?

When you watch television you may hear stories and see pictures of people fighting wars in other parts of the world.

A war is a violent argument between different groups of people.

Many people die because of war every year.

There is hardly ever a good reason
to turn a conflict into a fight.

And although sometimes adults think that they fight
for different or better reasons than children, often this
is not true.

We can all make our homes and classrooms and communities more peaceful by remembering a few simple rules.

Almost any fight can be avoided by learning to take turns, not calling names, not pushing somebody around just because you are bigger than them, and apologizing when you are wrong.

It is also important to listen to other people's opinions – even if they are different from yours. Make sure other people listen to your opinions, too.

Sometimes it is helpful to have a grown-up, or someone else who will not take sides, there to listen.

Once everyone has had their say
then you can begin to think
of different ways to solve the
problem together
peacefully.

Like so many things people do, learning to solve differences without fighting takes practice.

But if we all keep practicing, we really can make the world a more peaceful place.

# HOW TO USE THIS BOOK

Like all of life's tough lessons, learning how to resolve conflicts peacefully is an ongoing process. Many adults struggle with this idea and children, because of their limited experience in the world, need patience and strong support as they explore better ways of resolving their differences. Before talking with your child about conflict consider these thoughts:

Peaceful conflict resolution takes practice, just like learning to swim or practicing the piano. Be patient.

Children learn to resolve conflicts by watching others – especially adults. Fights between parents or other adults, and the way that parents react to children's fights, set the example. So take some time to think about how you resolve conflicts in your own life. If your tendency is to fight or be aggressive, you can hardly blame your children for reacting in the same way.

Teach your children that sometimes it is okay to get angry. But also teach them that there are both acceptable and unacceptable ways to express anger. Help your child to learn and know that peacefulness is more than just avoiding anger and violence. Explain that it doesn't mean that people never get mad or act impulsively. It means that people know how to talk to each other, appreciate each other's differences, and have a basic willingness to cooperate and compromise. It's even okay to "agree to disagree." Not all conflicts are worked through; most are

worked around. Let children discuss how they feel about fighting that they see on television and in the newspapers. Answer their questions as honestly as you can and try to bring world and local news stories down to their level of understanding. Sadly, most wars are fought for exactly the same reasons that children fight in the playground.

In larger classes it can be hard for teachers to find the time to help children resolve conflicts. Punishment and separating those involved often takes the place of talking things through. However, school is a major source of role models for children and whatever a teacher can do to help promote a dialogue between children is important.

Teachers can help by making children aware of the level of peacefulness in the classroom. You can talk about fighting in weekly discussions, and link it into specific topics (e.g., ancient civilizations such as the Romans).

Try making a "peace thermometer" with sunny skies and no clouds for a peaceful, cooperative day; clouds and wind indicating a day where people are using angry words and insults; storms for hitting and shoving; and hurricanes indicating major conflicts in class. String a bead through a long piece of string and tape each end to the thermometer. Slide the bead up and down depending on how things are going in the class. Give rewards, such as stickers, for peaceful days. If things are going badly, let the children make suggestions about how to bring the blue skies back.

## GLOSSARY

**aggression**  Hostile or threatening behavior.

**ashamed**  To feel embarrassed or bad about something you have done.

**community/communities**  A group of people who live or work in the same area.

**opinion**  The ideas and beliefs that a person has about something, usually based on his or her own life experiences.

**solve**  To find the answer to a problem.

## BOOKS TO READ

*And to Think That We Thought That We'd Never Be Friends* by Mary Ann Hoberman (Crown Publishers, 1999)

*Dealing With Anger (The Conflict Resolution Library)* by Marianne Johnston (Powerkids PR, 1998)

*Dealing With Fighting (The Conflict Resolution Library)* by Marianne Johnston (Powerkids PR, 1998)

*Hot Stuff to Help Kids Chill Out: The Anger Management Book* by Jerry Wilde (Lgr Productions, 1997)

*Peace Tales* by Margaret Read MacDonald (Linnet Books, 1992)

*Somewhere Today: A Book of Peace* by Shelley Moore Thomas and Eric Futran (Albert Whitman & Co., 2002)

*The Story of Ferdinand* by Munro Leaf (Viking Press, 1989)

*We Can Work It Out: Conflict Resolution for Children* by Barbara Kay Polland (Tricycle PR, 2000)

*Why Are You Fighting, Davy?* by Brigitte Weninger (North-South Books, 1999)

### For Parent and Adults

*Raising a Thinking Child: Help Your Child to Resolve Everyday Conflicts and Get Along With Others* by Myrna B. Shure and Theresa Foy Digeronimo (Pocket Books, 1996)